KIDS TRAVEL GUIDE TO
The Fun and Most Interesting Way To Discover and Explore Paris With Your Kids as a Family (Including Lovely Pictures of the City of Lights)

Williams Bryant

Table of Content

WELCOME TO PARIS (City of Lights)

Welcome to the magical city of Paris! Bursting with history, beauty, and excitement, Paris is a dream destination for adventurers like you. Get ready to embark on a journey through time and discover the wonders that await you in the City of Light.

Paris, the capital of France, is located in the heart of Europe. It is known for its iconic landmarks, charming streets, and vibrant atmosphere. With a history dating back over 2,000 years, this city has witnessed the rise and fall of empires, the birth of art and literature, and the shaping of world history.

One of the most famous symbols of Paris is the Eiffel Tower. Standing tall at 1,050 feet, this iron marvel offers breathtaking views of the city and is a must-visit for anyone coming to Paris. Did you know that the Eiffel Tower was built for the World's Fair in 1889 and was initially meant to be temporary? But Parisians fell in love with it, and it has become an enduring symbol of the city.

Another iconic site you'll encounter in Paris is the Louvre Museum. It is the world's largest art museum and is home to the famous painting, the Mona Lisa, among countless other masterpieces. You'll be amazed by the incredible art collections spanning thousands of years of human creativity.

Paris is also famous for its beautiful cathedrals, including the Notre-Dame Cathedral, which took almost 200 years to complete. Unfortunately, it suffered a devastating fire in 2019, but efforts are underway to restore its grandeur. The Cathedral of Notre-Dame is a masterpiece of Gothic architecture and holds a special place in the hearts of Parisians.

When it comes to food, Paris is a paradise for your taste buds! French cuisine is renowned around the world, and here you'll have the chance to try delicious pastries like croissants and macaroons, mouthwatering cheese, and maybe even escargots (that's fancy French for snails!). Don't forget to try a famous French baguette from a local bakery and enjoy a picnic in one of Paris' beautiful parks.

Paris is also a city of arts and culture. It has been home to many famous writers, artists, and musicians throughout history. You can explore the neighborhood of Montmartre, known for its bohemian atmosphere and the Sacré-Cœur Basilica. Visit the Latin Quarter and lose yourself in its charming streets filled with book shops and cafes.

In Paris, you'll experience a blend of history, culture, and the joy of discovery. From climbing the Eiffel Tower to strolling along the Seine River, every corner of this enchanting city has something to offer. So get ready to make lifelong memories and let the adventure begin!

Remember to keep this travel guide handy as we delve deeper into the wonders of Paris, providing you with exciting activities, fascinating stories, and helpful tips to make your journey an unforgettable one. Happy travels!

TOP ATTRACTIONS IN PARIS

The Eiffel Tower

The Eiffel Tower

The Eiffel Tower is undoubtedly one of the most exciting attractions in Paris, and it's a place where kids and adults alike can have a blast. Let's dive into the history and the fun things to see and do there.

History

The Eiffel Tower was indeed built by the French engineer Gustave Eiffel and completed in 1889.

The Eiffel Tower Under Construction

Gustave Eiffel, along with his team of engineers, designed and oversaw the construction of the tower. It was a remarkable engineering feat of its time, standing at a height of 1,050 feet (or about 320 meters) and comprising over 18,000 individual iron pieces held together by more than 2.5 million rivets.

The primary purpose of the Eiffel Tower was to serve as the entrance arch for the 1889 Exposition Universelle (World's Fair) held in Paris. The fair was organized to commemorate the 100th anniversary of the French Revolution and showcase technological advancements and cultural achievements.

When the Eiffel Tower was first unveiled, it received mixed reactions from the public. Some people admired its innovative design and grandeur, while others found it unusual and even criticized it as an eyesore. However, over time, the tower grew in popularity and became an integral part of the Parisian skyline. Today, it is celebrated as an architectural masterpiece and a beloved symbol of the city.

Originally, it was planned to be a temporary structure, intended to stand for only 20 years. However, due to its growing popularity and the tower's valuable communication functions (it served as a radio transmission tower), it was allowed to remain standing after the expiration of its original permit. Eventually, it became a cherished landmark and a symbol of Parisian pride.

Since its construction, the Eiffel Tower has witnessed numerous historic events and served various purposes. It played a crucial role during both World Wars, serving as a strategic communications center and, at times, as a lookout post. Today, it stands as an enduring testament to human ingenuity and an iconic attraction that attracts millions of visitors each year.

The Eiffel Tower's unique design, intricate ironwork, and its panoramic views of Paris continue to captivate the imaginations of people, young and old, making it a must-visit destination for anyone exploring the wonders of the city of Paris.

What to See and Do

When you visit the Eiffel Tower, you'll be amazed by its towering height and intricate ironwork. Here are some highlights that you won't want to miss:

Observation Decks: The Eiffel Tower has multiple observation decks that provide stunning views of Paris from different heights. Take an elevator ride up to the top and get ready to be awe-struck by the breathtaking panorama. On clear days, you can see famous landmarks like the Louvre Museum, Notre-Dame Cathedral, and the River Seine.

A beautiful View of the Eiffel Tower

Gustave Eiffel's Office: Explore a replica of Gustave Eiffel's office, located on the top floor. Step into the past and imagine what it would have been like for him to work on this engineering marvel. You can even see wax statues of Gustave Eiffel and Thomas Edison, who visited him there.

The History of the Eiffel Tower: Learn about the fascinating history of the tower through interactive exhibits. Discover how it was built, the challenges faced by the engineers, and the role it played in the World's Fair. It's a chance to delve into the past and understand the significance of this iconic landmark.

Dining Options: If you're feeling hungry, you can enjoy a meal or a snack at one of the restaurants or cafés on the Eiffel Tower. Imagine dining with a spectacular view of Paris spread out beneath you—it's a truly magical experience.

Tips for Visiting

- Purchase tickets in advance: The Eiffel Tower can get quite crowded, so it's a good idea to book your tickets online ahead of time. This way, you can skip the long lines and save time.
- Choose the right time: Consider visiting early in the morning or later in the evening to avoid the biggest crowds. The tower is especially beautiful at sunset when the city lights begin to twinkle.
- Take the stairs (if you can): If you're up for a bit of adventure and exercise, you can choose to

climb the stairs instead of taking the elevator. It's a unique way to experience the tower and also helps avoid long elevator queues.

- Bring a camera: Don't forget to capture the memories! The Eiffel Tower offers countless photo opportunities, so be sure to bring your camera or smartphone to snap some amazing shots.

Visiting the Eiffel Tower is an unforgettable experience that will leave you with memories to cherish forever. Soak in the incredible views, learn about its history, and make sure to have fun exploring one of the most iconic structures in the world!

The Louvre Museum

The Louvre Museum is a treasure trove of art and history, and it's an incredible place for kids to explore. Let's delve into its history, what to see and do there, and some tips for visiting:

History

The Louvre Museum does have a rich and fascinating history. Here are some additional details about its historical background:

The Louvre Museum

The Louvre Museum's history dates back to the 12th century when it was initially constructed as a fortress known as the Louvre Castle. It was built by King Philip II of France in 1190 as a defensive structure to protect the city of Paris. Over the centuries, the fortress underwent numerous expansions and modifications, transforming it into a grand royal palace.

During the Renaissance, several French kings, including Francis I and Louis XIV, expanded the Louvre into an opulent residence, showcasing their power and wealth. The palace became a center of arts and culture, housing the royal art collections and hosting extravagant events.

In 1793, during the French Revolution, the Louvre was repurposed as a public museum, following the decree by the National Convention. This decision was made with the intent of making art accessible to the general public and to create a space for education and inspiration. The museum opened its doors with a collection of approximately 500 paintings.

Over the years, the Louvre Museum expanded its collection through acquisitions, donations, and archaeological excavations. The museum played a crucial role in promoting and preserving art and cultural heritage. Today, it is renowned as the world's largest art museum and one of the most visited cultural institutions.

The Louvre Museum houses an astounding collection of artworks, encompassing various periods and civilizations. From ancient Egyptian artifacts to

Renaissance masterpieces, from Asian art to European sculptures, the museum offers a comprehensive journey through human artistic expression.

In addition to its permanent collection, the Louvre also hosts temporary exhibitions, showcasing special themes or highlighting specific artists. These exhibitions provide visitors with the opportunity to explore diverse artistic movements and gain a deeper understanding of different cultures.

The Louvre Museum stands as a testament to the enduring power of art and the importance of preserving our collective heritage. Its history as a fortress turned royal palace turned public museum represents the evolution of cultural institutions and the democratization of art. It continues to inspire and captivate visitors of all ages, making it a top attraction for kids and adults alike.

What to See and Do

The Louvre Museum is home to an astonishing array of art and historical artifacts from various civilizations. Here are some highlights that kids will enjoy:

- **Mona Lisa**

Picture of Mona Lisa on the Wall

One of the most famous paintings in the world, the Mona Lisa by Leonardo da Vinci, resides in the Louvre. Seeing this enigmatic masterpiece up close is an incredible experience. Kids can join the crowd to catch a glimpse of her enigmatic smile, but it's good to remember that there might be a bit of a crowd.

- **Venus de Milo**

Venus de Milo Statue

Aphrodite, known as the "Venus de Milo" (100 BC, Cyclades, Greece). Venus de Milo was discovered in 1820. She was found on the island of Melos in the south-western Cyclades. The big question behind this

19

piece is… Is it Aphrodite, who was often portrayed half-naked? Or can it be the sea goddess Amphitrite, who was venerated on Melos? You decide. This piece is located in room 346 on the ground floor in the Sully wing. She is in the Greek, Etruscan, and Roman Antiquities section of the museum.

- **Moai Sculpture**

Picture of Moai Statue

This piece is a head portion of a Moai sculpture. This is originally from Easter Island. You will find it in the Pavillon des Sessions. This piece is truly breathtaking. You will be in awe as it takes your breath away momentarily being in its presence.

- **Great Sphinx of Tanis**

Great Sphinx of Tanis

The Sphinx is a creature with the body of a lion and the head of a king. This is the largest Spinx outside of Egypt. You can find this on the ground floor in the Sully wing room 338.

The sphinx was inscribed with the names of the pharaohs Ammenemes II (12th Dynasty, 1929-1895 BC), Merneptah (19th Dynasty, 1212-02 BC) and Shoshenq I (22nd Dynasty, 945-24 BC). According to archaeologists, certain details suggest that this sphinx dates to an earlier period - the Old Kingdom (c. 2600 BC).

- **Horus**

These statues represent Horus in a hybrid form. He is depicted as a man with the head of a falcon. This statue depicts Horus holding the vase containing the ritual water in his raised hands; this vase is now missing. This piece is located in the Sully Wing ground floor room 334. I particularly enjoy the way the shadow plays a part in viewing this piece.

- **Egyptian Antiquities**

Explore the fascinating world of ancient Egypt. The Louvre houses an extensive collection of Egyptian artifacts, including mummies, hieroglyphs, and monumental statues. Kids can learn about pharaohs, gods, and the captivating stories of this ancient civilization.

- **Pyramid created by I.M. Pei's**

Picture of Louvre Pyramid at Night

One of the most iconic symbols outside of the Louvre stands the Pyramid created by I.M. Pei's.The pyrmaid was designed as the main entrance to the museum. Its transparent steel and glass framework allows visitors to admire the palace facades from the lobby beneath.

Tips for Visiting

- Plan ahead: The Louvre Museum is vast, and it's a good idea to plan which artworks or exhibits you'd like to see in advance. Pick a few highlights that interest your kids the most to make the most of your visit.
- Use a map or guide: The Louvre can be overwhelming due to its size. Grab a map or rent an audio guide to help navigate through the museum and find your way to the must-see artworks.
- Take breaks: The Louvre is a massive museum, and exploring it can be tiring. Take regular breaks, find seating areas, or enjoy a snack in one of the museum's cafes to rest and recharge.
- Interactive activities: The Louvre offers special activities and workshops for kids, such as treasure hunts or art-making sessions. Check the museum's website or inquire at the information desk to see if any special activities are available during your visit.

Visiting the Louvre Museum is an extraordinary journey through art and history. With its vast collection and captivating exhibits, it's sure to spark the imagination of young minds and create lasting memories. So get ready to embark on a fascinating adventure within the walls of this world-renowned museum!

Disneyland Paris

Disneyland Paris

Disneyland Paris, also known as Euro Disney, is a world-renowned theme park located in Marne-la-Vallee, a suburb of Paris, France. It is a top attraction for kids and families, offering a magical experience filled with beloved Disney characters, thrilling rides, enchanting shows, and immersive themed lands. Here is some information about Disneyland Paris, including its history, what to see and do there, and some tips for visiting.

History

Disneyland Paris

Disneyland Paris, originally known as Euro Disneyland, was inspired by the success of Disneyland in California and Walt Disney World in Florida. The idea of a European Disney theme park was conceived in the late 1970s, and after extensive planning and negotiations, construction began in 1988.

When Disneyland Paris opened on April 12, 1992, it faced some initial challenges. There were cultural differences, financial difficulties, and a lack of understanding of European visitors' preferences. However, the park underwent significant changes and improvements to better cater to the European audience.

In 1994, the park's name was changed from Euro Disneyland to Disneyland Paris to better reflect its location. Despite the challenges, Disneyland Paris gradually gained popularity and became a beloved destination for families and Disney enthusiasts from around the world.

In 2002, the second park, Walt Disney Studios Park, was opened adjacent to Disneyland Park. This park offers a different experience, focusing on the world of cinema and entertainment.

Disneyland Paris has continued to expand and enhance its offerings over the years. New attractions, themed lands, and entertainment options have been introduced to provide a memorable experience for visitors. The resort now includes multiple Disney-themed hotels, such as the Disneyland Hotel, Disney's Hotel New York, and Disney's Newport Bay Club, among others.

In addition to the parks and hotels, the resort features Disney Village, a lively shopping, dining, and entertainment district where visitors can find a variety of restaurants, shops, and entertainment venues. There's also Golf Disneyland, a 27-hole golf course for enthusiasts of the sport.

Today, Disneyland Paris remains one of Europe's top tourist destinations, offering a magical and immersive Disney experience with its iconic characters, enchanting attractions, and spectacular entertainment.

What to See and Do

Disneyland Park: This park is divided into five enchanting lands. **Main Street, U.S.A**. A nostalgic street with shops and dining. **Adventureland. Explore** exotic jungles and embark on thrilling adventures. **Frontierland.** Experience the Wild West with cowboys and gold rush themes. **Fantasyland.** Enter a realm of fairy tales and meet classic Disney characters. **Discoveryland.** Discover futuristic attractions and space-themed adventures.

Walt Disney Studios Park: This park offers a behind-the-scenes look at the magic of Disney movies and television. Key highlights include:

Toon Studio: Experience animation and meet beloved characters like Mickey and Buzz Lightyear.

Production Courtyard: Enjoy live shows and attractions inspired by Disney films.

Backlot: Discover movie sets and exciting rides like Ratatouille: The Adventure.

Entertainment: Disneyland Paris offers spectacular parades, fireworks, and live shows throughout the day. Don't miss the iconic Disney Stars on Parade and the nighttime extravaganza, Disney Illuminations.

Meet Disney Characters: Kids can meet and take photos with their favorite Disney characters at designated meet-and-greet locations throughout the parks.

Tips for Visiting

- Plan ahead: Check the official Disneyland Paris website for park hours, showtimes, and ride closures. Consider purchasing tickets online in advance to save time and avoid long queues at the entrance.
- FastPass: Utilize the FastPass system, which allows you to reserve a time slot for popular attractions and reduce wait times.
- Dress comfortably: Wear comfortable shoes and dress appropriately for the weather. Be prepared

for varying temperatures and consider bringing ponchos or umbrellas in case of rain.

- Bring snacks and water: While there are numerous dining options available, packing snacks and water can help keep kids energized between meals.
- Take breaks: Disneyland Paris can be overwhelming, so take regular breaks to rest and recharge. There are designated relaxation areas throughout the parks.
- Stay on-site: Consider staying at one of the themed Disney hotels to fully immerse yourself in the magical experience and enjoy perks like Extra Magic Hours, where hotel guests can enter the park before it opens to the public.
- Use child-friendly facilities: Disneyland Paris offers baby care centers, stroller rentals, and child swap services for families with young children.

Remember to check for any updated information and guidelines, as park policies may change over time. Enjoy your visit to Disneyland Paris, where dreams really do come true!

The Catacombs of Paris

The Catacombs of Paris

The Catacombs of Paris is an intriguing and unique attraction that may not be suitable for all kids due to its dark and somber nature. However, for older children with an interest in history and a sense of adventure, it can be a captivating experience. Here's some information about the Catacombs, including its history, what to see and do, and tips for visiting:

History

The Catacombs of Paris were created as a solution to the overcrowded cemeteries in the late 18th century. Here's some additional information about the history of the Catacombs:

During the late 18th century, Paris faced a significant problem with its cemeteries. The city's cemeteries, such as Saints-Innocents Cemetery, had become overcrowded, resulting in unsanitary conditions and potential health hazards. The solution came in the form of utilizing the extensive network of tunnels and quarries that existed beneath the city.

The transformation of the quarries into an ossuary began in 1785. The bones and remains from various cemeteries were exhumed and transported to the underground tunnels. The transfer of bones took place over several years and involved a careful and organized process of moving the remains.

The bones were arranged in a systematic manner within the Catacombs, creating haunting displays that are now visited by tourists. The catacombs stretch for approximately 2 kilometers (1.2 miles) and are located around 20 meters (66 feet) below ground level.

Initially, access to the Catacombs was limited, and only a few individuals, such as the Parisian elite, had the privilege to visit. However, in 1809, the Catacombs were opened to the public, and they have since become a unique and popular attraction in Paris, drawing visitors from around the world.

The Catacombs provide a chilling reminder of the city's history and the challenges it faced with burial practices in the past. They serve as a solemn and eerie memorial to the countless individuals whose remains were transferred there.

Visiting the Catacombs allows visitors to delve into this dark and fascinating part of Parisian history and offers a unique perspective on the city's past burial practices and the impact of overcrowding in cemeteries.

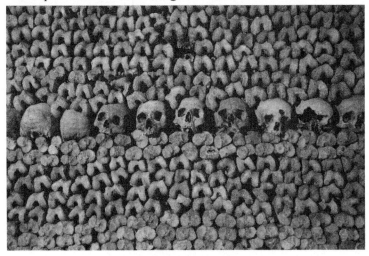

Bone structure in the Catacombs of Paris

What to See and Do

Walk through the underground passages: Visitors can explore a small section of the extensive network of tunnels that make up the Catacombs. The tour takes you along dimly lit corridors, showcasing walls lined with neatly arranged human bones.

Admire the bone displays: The catacombs feature carefully arranged bones and skulls, creating eerie and macabre displays. It's a fascinating sight that offers a unique perspective on the history of burial practices.

Learn about the history and significance: Informational panels are placed throughout the Catacombs, providing insights into the history and purpose of the underground ossuary. There are also audio guides available in multiple languages to enhance the experience.

Tips for Visiting

- Age restrictions: The Catacombs may not be suitable for young children or those who are sensitive to dark and confined spaces. It's advisable to consider the maturity and interests of your children before deciding to visit.
- Be prepared for limited facilities: The Catacombs do not have restrooms or refreshment facilities underground. It's a good idea to use the restroom and bring water and snacks before entering.

- Dress appropriately: The Catacombs maintain a cool temperature throughout the year, so it's advisable to wear comfortable clothing and sturdy shoes. The pathways can be uneven, so closed-toe shoes are recommended.
- Expect long queues: The Catacombs are a popular attraction, and long queues are common. Arriving early or purchasing tickets in advance can help minimize wait times.
- Respect the solemn atmosphere: The Catacombs are a place of remembrance and should be treated with respect. Visitors should maintain a quiet and solemn demeanor while exploring the underground tunnels.
- Follow the rules: There are specific rules and regulations in place to protect the Catacombs and ensure the safety of visitors. It's essential to adhere to these guidelines, including not touching the bones or straying from designated paths.

Visiting the Catacombs can be a unique and educational experience for older children with an interest in history and a capacity to appreciate the somber nature of the site. However, it's crucial to assess the appropriateness of the visit based on your child's age, maturity, and sensitivity to such environments.

Fun Facts About The Paris Catacombs

Visiting the Catacombs of Paris is a must-do for any traveler's bucket list. With guided tours available (which I highly recommend), you can explore this extensive and eerie burial site. However, it is not for the faint of heart. Once you descend several feet underground, you will be met with mounds of bones and piles of centuries-old skeletons, which may be too shocking for some. Additionally, if you have claustrophobia, necrophobia, or any underlying health issues, you may want to reconsider visiting this place.

If you are still curious about the Catacombs and want to learn more before your visit, here are some interesting and weird facts about them that you and your kids can explore. To make the most of your experience, I suggest booking a skip-the-line ticket to avoid long queues, or even better, a guided tour to access some restricted areas and learn more about the history of the Catacombs.

- *The Catacombs Are Bigger Than You May Think.*

One of the most interesting facts about the Catacombs of Paris is their sheer size. It is said that they span 300 km (185 miles) or even 500 km (310 miles) and cover an area of 11,000 square metres. They are also around 20 meters (65 feet) deep, which is close to the height of a 5-story building. Plus, there are close to 250 steps to go up and down. All in all, the Catacombs are huge and some parts of them remain unexplored.

- ### *It Wasn't Always Called Catacombs.*

The Paris Catacombs weren't always known by this name. Initially, it was the Paris Municipal Ossuary, consecrated on April 7, 1786. This was due to the need to move the remains from the largest cemetery in Paris, which had to be closed in 1780 due to space constraints. Later on, people fascinated with the Roman catacombs started referring to this site as catacombs too.

- ### *The Catacombs Were Previously Limestone Quarries.*

Before becoming a burial site, the area was a bunch of mines called the Tombe-Issoire quarries. A particular kind of limestone, known as Lutetian limestone, was mined from it and used for various buildings in Paris (like the Louvre museum, Les Invalides, etc) around the 15th and 16th centuries. When the quarries ran out of stones, the shafts were abandoned.

- ### *Some Parts Of The Catacombs Are Not Open To Visitors.*

Due to their extensive depth, the catacombs cannot be fully explored. In fact, many areas within it have restricted access and are difficult to get to. The part open to the public is called the Denfert-Rochereau Ossuary, which forms a small area of the entire catacomb network. However, there is a community of enthusiasts who like exploring the catacombs called cataphiles. They frequently traverse them as much as they can, sometimes even exploring the parts blocked off/not open to the public. Please note that these parts are not safe and should not be explored.

- ***There Are More People Buried There Than Alive In Paris.***

The largest cemetery in Paris at the time, the Holy Innocents' cemetery, had over 2 million remains buried in it. When the remains were excavated and moved into the quarries, other cemeteries with space constraints also moved the bodies into these mine shafts. Eventually, the bodies started piling up and the last count is said to be over 6 million bodies, which is much more than the 2 million people living in Paris.

Hence, there are more dead people beneath the city than living people above ground. If this isn't one of the spookiest facts about the Paris catacombs, then I don't know what is.

- ***Famous people have been visiting the ossuary since it opened to the public in 1809.***

To keep track of the number of visitors, a register was kept at the entrance. Some of the famous people who visited were the former King of France, Charles X (Count of Artois), the former Austrian emperor, Francis

I, and Napoleon III with his son. There's even a Gate of Hell below the catacombs, which was named after the street Rue d'Enfer, known for its nefarious activities. The last bones and remains to be put in the catacombs were in 1860. After 1810, the bones were arranged in creative displays, like artworks. In 1809, the catacombs were opened to the public, but only with prior permission and a few times a year. Now, they're open throughout the year and welcome all kinds of visitors. If you want to explore this peculiar place, you can purchase a skip-the-line entry ticket with an audio guide or opt for a guided tour to learn more about its history.

- *During World War II, the Paris Catacombs were utilized as underground tunnels by the French Resistance.*

This is one of the most interesting facts about the catacombs of Paris. The Resistance saw the Catacombs as an ideal hiding spot due to the hidden pathways and tunnels. It was also discovered that the Germans had set up bunkers in the Catacombs, with tents from both parties being located close to one another.

- *A large area of the capital is built on top of the underground tunnels of the Catacombs, the extent of which is unknown.*

In the 1700s-1800s, reckless construction was taking place across the city, resulting in sections of the city collapsing into the ground. In response, the French government declared that no tall buildings would be constructed in the city, particularly near the Catacombs, and that all structures would have a weight restriction.

- *The Catacombs were previously used as mines, with miners digging further in different directions to unearth more stones.*

As a result, a maze of unmapped tunnels was created. Jean Talairach and René Suttel explored the Catacombs in 1938 and mapped as much as they could, but they were unable to cover the entire area. This map was later donated to the French Resistance to help them use the Catacombs as a hideout and coordinate the battle more effectively..

- *Apart from being used as burial grounds, the Catacombs of Paris have also been used for entertainment purposes.*

This is something that cataphiles, or people who explore the Catacombs, have been doing for years. In 2004, a group of policemen undergoing training stumbled upon a surprise discovery - equipment that suggested people were hosting parties in the Catacombs. This included a restaurant, bar, lounge, and even a makeshift cinema theater with a projector and seats carved into the stones! Wires were also used to siphon off electricity to power the devices.

- *In addition, the tunnels have also been used to host temporary exhibitions such as The Dead of the French Revolution and Skeleton Story.*

The Paris Catacombs receive between 350,000 and 550,000 visitors each year, and since it became a popular attraction in Paris, people have been visiting since it opened to the public.

- *One of the lesser-known facts about the Catacombs is that a movie was filmed there.*

As Above, So Below, a horror movie released in 2014, was the first film to be granted permission to film in the Catacombs. After getting the go-ahead from the French authority, the Paris Catacombs were used as the filming location and much of it was portrayed in the movie as it is in the Catacombs.

Parc Des Buttes Chaumont

Parc Des Buttes Chaumont

Parc des Buttes Chaumont is a beautiful and family-friendly park located in the northeastern part of

Paris, France. It offers a serene escape from the bustling city and provides a range of activities for kids. Here's some information about the park's history, what to see and do, and tips for visiting with children:

History

A Beautiful View of Parc Des Buttes Chaumont

Parc des Buttes Chaumont in Paris was designed by landscape architect Jean-Charles Alphand and opened in 1867.

Parc des Buttes Chaumont was part of a major urban planning project in the mid-19th century to create green spaces and parks throughout Paris. The park was built on a site that was once occupied by gypsum quarries and a landfill, making its transformation into a picturesque landscape all the more remarkable.

Under the direction of Alphand, the former quarries were shaped into hills and cliffs, and the landfill was reworked to create a large central lake. The park's layout followed the English garden style, characterized by meandering paths, rolling hills, and artificial rock formations.

One of the notable features of Parc des Buttes Chaumont is the Temple de la Sibylle, perched atop a rocky island in the middle of the lake. The temple, inspired by ancient Roman architecture, adds a touch of grandeur and serves as a focal point within the park.

The park's design aimed to provide a tranquil and picturesque retreat for Parisians, offering a contrast to the urban landscape. It quickly became a popular destination for residents seeking relaxation and natural beauty.

Over the years, Parc des Buttes Chaumont has undergone various improvements and additions. Additional plantings, including trees and flowers, have enhanced the park's aesthetic appeal. The original structures, such as pavilions and bridges, have been maintained and restored to preserve the park's historical character.

Today, Parc des Buttes Chaumont remains a beloved green space in Paris, attracting both locals and tourists. Its scenic landscapes, diverse plant life, and recreational facilities make it a popular destination for leisurely walks, picnics, and enjoying outdoor activities.

The park's history as a former quarry and landfill adds to its unique charm, serving as a reminder of its transformation into a beautiful urban oasis. Parc des Buttes Chaumont stands as a testament to the vision and expertise of its designer, Jean-Charles Alphand, and continues to be a cherished attraction for visitors of all ages.

What to See and Do

Explore the landscape: The park features diverse landscapes, including cliffs, waterfalls, lakes, and a man-made island. Kids can enjoy exploring the various paths, bridges, and hidden corners of the park.

Visit the Temple de la Sibylle: Perched on top of a rocky cliff, the Temple de la Sibylle is a striking feature of the park. It offers panoramic views of the surrounding area and provides a great photo opportunity.

Ride the carousel: Parc des Buttes Chaumont has a charming carousel with beautifully crafted animals. Kids can enjoy a nostalgic ride on the carousel and create lasting memories.

Boat on the lake: The park's central lake offers rowboat rentals during the summer months. Kids can enjoy a leisurely boat ride on the lake, taking in the park's scenic beauty.

Play in the playgrounds: Parc des Buttes Chaumont has multiple playgrounds designed for children of different age groups. These playgrounds offer swings, slides, climbing structures, and sandboxes, providing a fun-filled experience for kids.

Relax and picnic: The park has ample green spaces and picnic areas where families can unwind and enjoy a picnic surrounded by nature. It's a great opportunity to have a leisurely lunch and spend quality time together.

Tips for Visiting

- Plan for the weather: Check the weather forecast before visiting and dress accordingly. Bring hats, sunscreen, and water during hot summer days. In cooler months, bring extra layers to stay warm.
- Pack snacks and drinks: Although there are some food options available in the park, it's a good idea to bring snacks and drinks, especially for kids. This will help keep them energized and hydrated throughout the visit.
- Comfortable footwear: The park has hilly areas and pathways, so it's recommended to wear comfortable walking shoes. This will ensure a

more enjoyable experience for both kids and adults.

- Be mindful of safety: As with any public space, it's important to keep an eye on your children and ensure their safety. Stay within designated areas and supervise their activities.
- Take breaks: Parc des Buttes Chaumont is a vast park, and exploring it can be tiring, especially for younger children. Take breaks, sit on the benches, and let kids rest or play in the playgrounds when needed.
- Capture memories: Don't forget to bring a camera or smartphone to capture the beautiful scenery and memorable moments with your family.

Parc des Buttes Chaumont offers a peaceful and family-friendly atmosphere, making it an excellent choice for a day of outdoor fun and relaxation in Paris.

FOODS IN PARIS

I've said it before, but my main reason for choosing a destination for travel is often the foods on offer there – and Paris was no exception! Trying the amazing French food was high on my list of things to do in Paris, and getting to introduce my kids to some of those foods was something I was really looking forward to. If you have a trip planned and are looking for some great French foods to try in Paris with kids, this is a great place to start!
Baguettes

If you're a fan of carbs, then France is the right country to come for food. Bread in all forms is widely celebrated here, and none more so than the baguette; there's even a competition in Paris each year to find the best one! If you're looking for a popular French food to try with kids, then this is a great place to start; it's a familiar food, but one that Paris does especially well.

Baguettes

Freshly Baked Baguettes

Baguettes are sold in boulangeries around Paris; boulangeries are French bakeries and in order to hold the title "boulangerie" they must bake their bread on the premises. You want to ask for " la tradition" which will be the baker's own recipe for baguettes; different locations might be slightly different, but they should all be long and thin and fluffy and delicious!

Cheese

French Cheese

Cheese is my favorite food in the world, and given the choice I will almost always choose cheese to end a meal over a dessert. You'll often find cheese boards on French menus with the dessert choices, and it's a great way to try a number of different cheeses in one go.

Some French cheeses can be quite strong so for kids used to something a little milder, there are certain cheeses to start with. Camembert and Brie are soft cheeses that don't have too strong of a flavor, and are nice when spread on a slice of baguette. For children with a stronger palette, Roquefort is my favorite blue cheese with an amazing flavor.

Macarons

French Macarons

Macarons (not to be confused with macaroons, which are the more cakey, chewy cookie made with coconut) are said to have originally come to France from Italy, but these days they're more commonly associated with Paris. They've become super popular in the US so chances are that you've tried a macaron at some point – but they're especially delicious in Paris!

Patisseries are French pastry shops that employ master pastry chefs, and you'll find them all over Paris. These are the best places to find macarons, and you'll find them in a variety of pretty colors and flavors. They make a great gift to take back to friends back home, but they're very delicate so make sure they're packed carefully!

Crepes

Crepes with Sauce

Crepes are very thin pancakes that can be either sweet or savory. They make a great light lunch or a snack to eat on the go, and because the mild flavor is so similar to pancakes, most kids should be willing to give them a try when visiting France.

We found that most restaurants in Paris didn't have kids menus so we were always looking for lighter portions for kids so they could eat a manageable sized meal; crepes were perfect for this. I love the savory crepes filled with ham and cheese, but crepes filled with chocolate sauce or strawberry jam will probably be as popular with your kids as mine!

Frogs legs

You might want to save this one for older kids, or those with more adventurous tastes! I think frog legs actually taste a lot like chicken, but it's more the idea of them that people seem to struggle with. Plenty of Parisian restaurants will serve frog legs, so you just need to be brave enough to order them!

If your kids are up for trying frog legs, then another French food to try might be escargots. I've never been a huge fan unless they're doused in huge amounts of garlic butter, but they're a very traditional French food to try and some people love them!

Croque Monsieur

This is a great French food to try in Paris with kids because it's so familiar. A Croque Monsieur is essentially a ham and cheese toasted sandwich made with a béchamel sauce, and most kids are used to the flavors. When I was wondering what my very picky eater would eat in Paris, this was the one thing I knew he'd enjoy!

A Ham and Cheese Toasted Sandwich

You'll find these on the menu in most restaurants, and they make another great light option for kids. The flavors of the cheese can sometimes be a bit stronger than kids are used to, but other than that they're a great option for kids who want to try French food without straying too far from their comfort zone.

Éclairs

I don't think you can go wrong when it comes to French pastries, everything is beautiful and delicious and I would encourage you to try as many of them as possible! But my favorite has to be the éclair.

Picture of éclair

Éclairs are made with choux pastry and filled with patisserie cream or custard and then topped with an icing. My favorite are chocolate éclairs, which are usually filled with custard or chocolate cream and topped with chocolate icing. I had an amazing chocolate éclair at a café on the first level of the Eiffel Tower and whilst eating a chocolate éclair on the Eiffel Tower might be the most touristy thing ever, it was an unforgettable experience!

Steak Frites

This is another great French food to try in Paris with kids since it's literally just steak and fries and is something they're probably familiar with anyway. You can find these in Parisian brasseries, which are typically more casual places serving traditional French foods.

Steak Frites

I'm not usually a fan of steak, but the steak I had in Paris was amazing! The fries will usually be thin cut fries that most kids will probably like, so this is a great choice for picky eaters. If your kids are a bit more adventurous then look for steak frites with different sauces; the best I had was with a Roquefort sauce that was to die for!

Chocolate

There are some amazing chocolatiers in Paris, so finding somewhere to try incredible chocolate won't be too hard at all! Not many kids don't like chocolate (one of my children doesn't like it, but my other child more than makes up for it!) so sampling chocolates and chocolate dishes in Paris should be a popular activity!

Heart Shaped Chocolate

We visited Paris during a heatwave with record high temperatures so instead of buying chocolates, we opted for chocolate dishes on the menu. Chocolate mousse is a popular option, as well as chocolate soufflé. I don't think you can go wrong with any French dessert, but the chocolate ones are always my favorite!

Waffles

French Waffles

Waffles aren't something I would necessarily think of when talking about French food but we saw them on the menu so often in Parisian cafés that I had to include them on this list; not only are they a great French food for kids to try, but they were so good everywhere we tried them!

While you can just get waffles with powdered sugar, they're even better with chocolate! They make a great on the go snack or dessert after lunch, and are often big enough to be shared. Sitting in a café in Paris drinking coffee or hot chocolate with a warm chocolate waffle is an amazing experience!

RESTAURANTS IN PARIS

Casa Luca

Address: 82, Ave. Marceau, 75008 Paris
Contact Number: 01 47 20 20 40
Website: https://www.casaluca.fr/
Cuisine: Italian

A quaint trattoria featuring authentic Italian charcuterie and a view of the Arc de Triomphe.

Openings: Breakfast, Lunch & Dinner daily, Brunch Sun. Open every day from 12:00 pm to 11:00 pm and on weekends until 11:30 pm.

Features

- *Air conditioning*
- *Dress code: Business casual*
- *Full bar*
- *Kid-friendly*
- *Outdoor dining*

Casa Luca Restaurant

The young and dashing owner of this elegant trattoria, Nicolas Richard, proposes a modern and comfortable ambience equipped with cozy, dark pink seats, chic wooden tables, and a roaring fireplace.

Casa Luca, Paris, France.

Just a few steps away from the iconic Arc de Triomphe on the chic Avenue Marceau, La Casa is an Italian restaurant with a cozy and inviting atmosphere. The interior was designed by renowned architect Pierre-Yves Rochon, who is also responsible for the renovations of the George-V and Shangri-La hotels.

What makes La Casa stand out is the children's cooking workshops that take place every Sunday at noon. While parents enjoy a delicious brunch, kids are given the opportunity to make pizzas, cakes and other dishes. Everyone is then invited to sit down and enjoy the meal together.

<u>Breakfast in America</u>

Address: 17, rue des Ecoles, 75005 Paris;
4, rue Malher, 75004 Paris.
Contact Number: 01 43545028; 01 42724021
Website: https://breakfast-in-america.com/
Cuisine: American / Breakfast / Burgers

American-style diner serving breakfast, burgers and more.

Openings: Open daily 8:30 a.m.-11 p.m.

Features

- *Dress code: Casual*
- *Kid-friendly*

Breakfast in America, Paris.

Craig Carlson, the owner of Breakfast in America, created the restaurant out of his nostalgia for the morning meals of his homeland. The menu features a variety of breakfast items such as scrambled eggs, omelets, and pancakes, as well as lunchtime favorites like burgers, club sandwiches, and wraps. For those with a sweet tooth, there are New York-style cheesecake, apple pie, and milkshakes. Beer and wine are also available.

La Coupole
Address: 102, bd du Montparnasse, 75014 Paris
Contact Number: 01 43 20 14 20
Website: http://www.lacoupoleparis.com/
Cuisine: Brasserie / Seafood / Breakfast
A Montparnasse landmark for shellfish assortments, grilled meats and carafes of sprightly house Riesling.
Openings: Breakfast, Lunch & Dinner daily. Open until 1:00am

Features
- Air conditioning
- Dress code: Casual
- Kid-friendly
- Outdoor dining
- Private room(s)

La Coupole Restaurant

La Coupole Restaurant Review:
This iconic Montparnasse destination, carefully restored and managed by the Flo brasserie group, has retained its allure. The menu reflects Flo's signature style, featuring generous platters of shellfish, grilled meats, and carafes of the house Riesling, all served by friendly waiters.

Le Grand Cafe
Address: 4, bd des Capucines, 75009 Paris
Contact Number: 01 43 12 19 00
Website: https://www.legrandcafe.com/
Cuisine: French / Brasserie
The extravagant décor is a replica of a Roaring Twenties café boulevardier.
Openings: Open 24 hours
Features

- *Air conditioning*
- *Dress code: Casual*
- *Kid-friendly*
- *Outdoor dining*

Le Grand Café Restaurant, Paris.

The server will not express any displeasure if you decide to order a single course, such as a shellfish assortment, onion au gratin soup, grilled sea bass with fennel, or steak tartare. The interior design is a faithful reproduction of a 1920s café boulevardier.

Mama Shelter

Address: 109, rue de Bagnolet, 75020 Paris

Contact Number: 01 43 48 48 48

Website:https://mamashelter.com/paris-east/eat-drin

k/

Cuisine: French / Breakfast

Modern hotel restaurant designed by Philippe Starck.

Openings: Lunch Mon.-Sat., Dinner nightly, Brunch Sun.

Features

- *Valet parking*
- *Air conditioning*
- *Dress code: Business casual*
- *Full bar*
- *Kid-friendly*
- *Outdoor dining*

Mama Shelter, Paris.

This stylish brasserie is furnished with sofas, chairs of all sizes and tables that lead guests to a very chic bar, decorated with "tables d'hôte" and painted armchairs. The low ceilings contribute to the overall atmosphere.

From the terrace, one can see the old railroad tracks reminiscent of Marcel Carné's pictures. This is not just a hotel restaurant, but a place where one can share a moment of hospitality and serenity with other guests. Chef Guy Savoy is in charge of the kitchen of the establishment. He offers signature dishes such as the saucisson de Lyon with pistachio and brioche and the bread-crumbed tuna with tonkatsu sauce. Green lentils salad with soft-boiled egg and the hearty Black Angus flank steak with homemade french fries and pepper sauce are also popular. Pair the food with a cocktail, such as the Hemingway daiquiri with rum, lime and grapefruit, or a glass of 2013 Côtes-du-Rhône Châteauneuf du Pape La Présidente. For dessert, indulge in the XL version of the Paris-Brest, a pastry filled with praline cream and sprinkled with almonds. This unique hotel and its restaurant with a totally original, modern and glamorous decor is the best work of Philippe Starck to date. À la carte, around €40.

ore (Palace of Versailles)
Address: Place d'Armes, 78000 Versailles
Contact Number: 01 30 84 12 96
Website:https://www.alain-ducasse.com/en/restaurant
/ore-ducasse-au-chateau-de-versailles
Cuisine: Café / French / Breakfast
Modern café from Alain Ducasse in the Palace of Versailles.

Openings: Open Tues.-Sun. 8 a.m.-6:30 p.m.

Features

- *Dress code: Casual*
- *Full bar*
- *Heart-healthy dishes*
- *Kid-friendly*
- *Private room(s)*

ore, Versailles, france

Alain Ducasse is the proprietor of this modern café situated in the Palace of Versailles. It is located on the first floor of the Pavillon Dufour, which is currently undergoing renovation. Stéphane Duchiron, a highly skilled chef who has previously worked at Les Fougères and Le Relais du Parc, is in charge of the kitchen. He has access to the finest ingredients, which he uses to create exquisite dishes with his cooking and seasoning expertise. The menu offers both simple items such as croque monsieur with ham and Comté cheese and more sophisticated dishes such as pumpkin velouté with croutons, raw salmon seasoned with pepper, juniper and lemon-flavored cream, spiced guinea fowl supreme and beef fillet with pan-seared foie gras and Anna potatoes. To top it off, the chocolate soufflé with vanilla sherbet is a delightful treat. Children are welcome and are provided with their own menu, as well as drawing and coloring materials. The staff is very courteous and the wine list is impressive, with around 50 labels, including a Pinot Noir Fournier 2014 by the glass.

Au Petit Riche

Address: 25, rue Le Peletier, 75009 Paris

Contact Number: 01 47 70 68 68

Website: https://www.restaurant-aupetitriche.com/

Cuisine: French / Bistro

This institution is a hangout for bankers and auctioneers as well as the after-theater crowd.

Openings: Lunch & Dinner daily, Open until midnight

Features

- *Dress code: Casual Dressy*
- *Kid-friendly*
- *Private room(s)*

restaurant au petit riche

This bistro, with its brass trim, mirrors, and woodwork, shines and glistens with nostalgia. It is a popular spot for bankers, auctioneers, and theater-goers, and still serves up delicious, hearty dishes such as coq au vin de Chinon, calf's head sauce gribiche, and sole meunière. The selection of Loire Valley wines is also excellent.

Pizza Pino

Address: 31/33, av. des Champs-Elysées, 75008 Paris
Contact Number: 01 40 74 01 12
Website: https://www.pizzapino.fr/
Cuisine: Italian / Pizza

Champs-Elysées outpost of this Italian pizza chain.

Openings: Lunch & Dinner daily Open from 11:30am to 5am.

Features

- *Air conditioning*

- *Dress code: Casual*
- *Kid-friendly*
- *Outdoor dining*

People Standing Outside Pizza Pino, Paris.

This Pizza Pino chain location offers pricey Italian cuisine. Enjoy a variety of pizzas, pastas, and salads while observing the hustle and bustle of the Champs-Elysées. The restaurant is open 24 hours a day, so you can drop in at any time.

Le Procope
Address: 13, rue de l'Ancienne-Comédie, 75006 Paris
Contact Number: 01 40 46 79 00
Website: https://www.procope.com/
Cuisine: French / Brasserie.

Paris' oldest café, dating back to the late seventeenth century.

Openings: Open daily until 1am

Features

- *Dress code: Casual*
- *Kid-friendly*
- *Outdoor dining*
- *Private room(s)*

Le Procope, Paris.

Established in 1686, the capital's oldest café has been restored to its original 17th century grandeur. However, it may not be the ideal place to enjoy a full meal. Tourists can be seen at the tables, indulging in the ordinary brasserie cuisine (shellfish, coq au vin).

Le Train Bleu (*Gare de Lyon*)

Address: 20, bd Diderot, 75012 Paris

Contact Number: 01 43 43 09 06

Website: https://www.le-train-bleu.com/fr/

Cuisine: French / Brasserie / Wine Bar

In the Gare de Lyon, this venerable vestige of the late nineteenth century promises a dazzling décor and satisfying classic French food.

Openings: Restaurant: Lunch 11:15 a.m.-2:30 p.m., Dinner 7 p.m.-10:30 p.m.; Bar Lounge: 7:30 a.m.-10:30 p.m.

Features

- *Parking available*
- *Dress code: Casual Dressy*
- *Full bar*
- *Kid-friendly*

Le Train Bleu Restaurant

At the Gare de Lyon, ascend the grand staircase to find a stunning restaurant where the visual feast is unparalleled. The décor is extravagant, colossal, delirious, and dazzling. Formerly, the food was not noteworthy, but now it is composed of classic dishes that are expertly prepared. If you are waiting for a train, visit the Big Ben bar for a drink and take advantage of the space. A variety of wines are available by the glass.

DRINKS IN PARIS

France is known all around the world for its wine production, but there are other drinks, hidden in the dark, that just want to come out. Together, let's go over all the regions of France to discover all those drinks good for your kids

- Oasis Orange

First of all, oasis is a fruit-flavored beverage. The very first drinks were all orange flavor, but with the success this brand had, other flavors are now available. It is a drink you should drink chilled in order to taste its delicious flavor.

- Fruit syrup and water

If a slice of lemon in your glass of water doesn't give your drink enough flavor, try a fruit syrup. France is known for its great variety of fruit syrup flavors, this way, you will be able to mix any type of syrup with water to give it even more flavor. Different brands of fruit syrup exist but the most popular one is named Teisseire.

- Diabolo

Diabolo is another soft drink with syrup in it. This drink is popular and refreshing. Diabolo is a mix of any type of syrup with pop. Add some ice and enjoy!

- Perrier

Perrier is a French sparkling mineral water which comes from a source located in Vergèze in the Gard. Perrier offers a different range of sparkling water, thereby offering a range of fine bubbles. Just as is the case with the mineral water, you can put a slice of lemon in your drink, or even some syrup. Mint syrup being the one the most associated with Perrier.

- Pop (French soda).

French homemade soda is a very refreshing drink, which is usually served in spring or during summer. You will find soda in any bar in France since it is a very popular drink.

- Apple Juice

Apple juice is the perfect alternative for those who don't drink alcohol, and therefore don't drink alcoholic cider, but still want to taste a delicious apple flavor. This juice can be served to children as well as adults.

- Grape Juice

France being one of the biggest wine producers, it is obvious that there is no shortage of grapes. In this way, when the grape isn't made into wine, it can be tasted as a juice. Grape juice is a delicious drink that is different from ordinary fruit juices.

- Lemonade (Pressed Lemon)

Pressed lemon is a popular drink in France. This is the type of drink you usually find at bars and in coffee shops. It is made of freshly squeezed lemon juice, a little bit of ice, some sugar, and some water. The ingredients are displayed in front of you so that you can weigh the ingredients yourself to fit your expectations.

- Orangina soda

Orangina is a sparkling drink with an orange flavor, which belongs to the company Orange Suntory France. This soda is very popular in France which many people drink. This soda is delicious when served cool. You can also serve it to children.

- Gini Soda

Gini is a French brand of soda. It is a sparkling drink with a lemon flavor. Just like Orangina, this soda should be served cool and is children-friendly. Gini has a totally different taste from a simple Perrier with lemon since Gini contains much more sugar.

- Breizh Cola

Breizh cola is a soda that comes from Brittany and is an excellent alternative to the well-known Coca-Cola. This soda will allow you to discover what the local production from the different regions of France are capable of.

- Hot Chocolate

We can't finish this list of typical French drinks without talking about hot chocolate.

This is a much needed, hot chocolate will always be present by your side.

OUTDOOR ACTIVITIES IN PARIS

Paris offers a wide range of fun activities for kids to enjoy, both outdoors and indoors. Here are some suggestions for activities that will keep kids entertained during a visit to the city:

Outdoor Activities

Parks and Gardens: Paris is home to numerous parks and gardens where kids can run, play, and enjoy the outdoors. Jardin du Luxembourg, Parc des Buttes Chaumont, and Jardin des Tuileries are just a few examples of parks with playgrounds, open spaces, and beautiful scenery.

Jardin des Tuileries (Tuileries Gardens)

Address: Place de la Concorde
75001 Paris.
Tel.. +33 (0) 1 40 20 53 17
Website: https://www.louvre.fr

The Tuileries Gardens take their name from the tile factories which were located on the site where Queen Catherine de Medici constructed the Palais des Tuileries in 1564. André Le Nôtre, the renowned gardener of King Louis XIV, redesigned the gardens in 1664 to give them their current French formal garden style. The gardens, which divide the Louvre from the Place de la Concorde, are a great spot for walking and for culture for Parisians and tourists; Maillol statues are placed alongside those of

Rodin or Giacometti. The gardens' two ponds are ideal places to relax. The Musée de l'Orangerie, where visitors can view the works of Monet, is in the south-west part of the Tuileries. From March to December, free tours in French are organized. Those who enjoy candyfloss and fairground rides will appreciate the Fête des Tuileries, from June to August.

Jardin des Tuileries (Tuileries Gardens)

Services and facilities of the establishment
- Gift shop
- Bookshop
- Restaurants

Restaurants: - **La Terrasse de Pomone** (open all year according to the time of the Jardin des Tuileries) - **Café des Marronniers** (opens from monday to sunday from 7am - 9pm) - **Restaurant Le Médicis** (Lunch 10.30am - 5pm and Dinner 5pm - 7pm)

Luxembourg Garden (Jardin du Luxembourg)
Address: Rue de Médicis - Rue de Vaugirard, 75006 Paris
Tel.. +33 (0) 1 42 64 33 99
Website: www.senat.fr/visite/jardin

Jardin du Luxembourg

Situated between Saint-Germain-des-Prés and the Latin Quarter, the Luxembourg Gardens were created in 1612 by Queen Marie de Medici, inspired by the Boboli Gardens in Florence. Spanning 25 hectares, the gardens are divided into French and English sections, with a geometric forest and a large pond in between. There is also an orchard with a variety of old and forgotten apples, an apiary, and greenhouses with a collection of orchids and a rose garden. The garden is home to 106 statues, the monumental Medici fountain, the Orangerie, and the Pavillon Davioud.

The Luxembourg Gardens offer a variety of activities and facilities for both children and adults. Children can enjoy puppets, rides, and slides, while adults can play chess, tennis, and bridge, or rent remote control boats. The cultural programme includes free photography exhibitions on the garden railings and concerts in the bandstand.

Educational activities include a crèche (2pm to 6pm) from May to mid-September for children aged 18 months to 6 years, a playground (open from 10am) for children aged 7 to 12 years, and a puppet theatre (Wednesdays, Saturdays, and Sundays from 2pm, and everyday from 4pm during the school holidays). Pony rides, swings, tennis, and model yacht hire are also available.

The Luxembourg Gardens also feature a restaurant, Madame's Terrace, as well as two refreshment stalls serving finger food to eat on the premises or take away. Several kiosks selling beverages, confectionery, food, and toys can be found in various parts of the garden.

Parc de Bercy

Address: 128 Quai de Bercy, 75012 Paris, France
Website: http://meslieux.paris.fr/

Situated on the site of former wine warehouses, the Parc de Bercy still retains some vestiges of its past, such as a vineyard and an old railway line. Located in the 12th arrondissement, between Gare de Lyon and the Cour Saint-Émilion district, the Parc de Bercy is a great place to take a stroll regardless of the season. On one side is the largest concert venue in Paris, Bercy Arena. At the other end is the 'jardin romantique' with its small lake and island, populated with ducks and lilies. In between, movie buffs visit the Cinémathèque française (designed by American architect Franck Gehry). Biodiversity is an important part of the Parc de Bercy, with the Maison du Lac (exhibitions on the gardens, conferences, etc.), the Maison du Jardinage (advice for new gardeners, gardening classes, etc.) the Chai de Bercy (wine store) and the Orangerie. The park is a popular spot for families to go for a walk, play football and rollerblade and is a great place for Parisians to relax.

France Miniature

Address: 25 route du Mesnil
78990 Élancourt
Tel.. +33 (0) 1 30 16 16 30
Email: info@franceminiature.com
Website: www.franceminiature.com

France Miniature offers a unique opportunity to explore the various regions of France. You can take a giant's stride around the Eiffel Tower, Vaux le Vicomte, St Tropez, Mont St Michel, the amphitheatre at Arles, the basilica of Lourdes, and many more. The journey doesn't end there! During your visit, you can visit the Palais de la Miniature (the miniature palace) where miniature characters live. To complete your visit, there is a play area for children. Your child can enjoy a six track toboggan, visit the panoramic tower and many other activities, all while taking in the scenery.

Villette Park

Address: 211 avenue, Jean Jaures,
75019 Paris, France
+33 140 03 75 75
Website: www.lavillette.com
Email: c.eppghv@villette.com

Villette Park, Paris.

The Parc de la Villette is a stunning green space in Paris, boasting 35 hectares of greenery and 3,000 m² of ecological gardens that promote biodiversity. This multi-disciplinary arts and culture venue is visited by more than 10 million people each year, and offers a variety of art, culture, scientific, educational, leisure and game activities. It is also home to 26 bright red 'follies' designed by Bernard Tschumi, each devoted to a different cultural or leisure activity. This vibrant spot is constantly being transformed, and it offers a packed programme of unexpected, innovative and often spectacular events. If you haven't yet explored this public space open to all, now is the perfect time to do so!

Belleville Park (Parc de Belleville)

Address: 47 rue des Couronnes
75020 Paris
+33 1 43 15 20 20
Website: http://meslieux.paris.fr/

Belleville, Paris.

In the 18th century, Belleville was nothing more than a rural area with farms, windmills, and open-air cafes. However, the former village, which became a home for people of modest means who were driven out of Paris by Haussman's renovations at the end of the 19th century, has recently undergone a dramatic transformation. Built in 1988 on top of the Belleville hill, the Belleville park (45,000 m²) offers an unrestricted view of the capital. It features a wooded village designed for children, with tower staircases and toboggans of all sizes, a water course with waterfalls and streams, and a panoramic viewpoint from which to admire the Parisian landscape. As a reminder of the area's wine-producing past, the park also has 140 vines, each of which yields around 2 to 3 kilos of grapes. Every year, the grapes are harvested.

Parc Andre Citroen

Address: 2 rue Cauchy
75015 Paris
Tel.. +33 1 53 98 73 84
Email: equipement.paris.fr

The Parc André Citroën is situated on the former Parisian Citroën factory grounds. It was opened in 1992 and covers an area of 14 hectares, making it one of the newest parks in the capital. This modern site, designed by renowned landscapers and architects (Alain Provost, Gilles Clément, Patrick Berger, Jean-Paul Viguier and François Jodry), offers a stunning view of the Seine and is the only green space in Paris that opens directly onto the river. The park is divided into three distinct areas: the Jardin Blanc, the Jardin Noir and the large central park area. Visitors can explore a variety of exotic trees and rare plants, two impressive hothouses and many other surprises. The park offers a range of facilities for relaxation or entertainment. Children can take advantage of the ball-games area, ping-pong tables, spring-based toys and toboggans, as well as the tethered air balloon offering a 150m high ride for children and adults (weather permitting).

Parc Des buttes chaumont

Address: 1-7 rue Botzaris
75019 Paris
Tel…+33 1 48 03 83 10
Website: http://meslieux.paris.fr/

Parc Des buttes chaumont

The Buttes-Chaumont Park, located in the north-east of Paris, is one of the largest and most unique green spaces in the city, covering an area of 25 hectares. Its construction on former quarries has resulted in its impressive steepness and changes in elevation. Visitors can enjoy breathtaking views of the city from this hilly landscape, particularly in the Montmartre district. The park's layout is particularly charming, featuring caves, waterfalls, a suspended bridge, and a high viewpoint. It is also adorned with exotic and native trees, and a variety of birds, such as seagulls, moorhens, and mallard ducks, can be seen in the area, as well as an artificial lake. There are also entertainment options for children, and places to get food and take a break.

Parc Monceau

Address: 35 boulevard de Courcelles
75008 Paris
Website: http://meslieux.paris.fr/

Parc Monceau, Paris.

Parc Monceau was constructed in the 17th century, under the orders of the Duke of Chartres. Located in the 8th arrondissement, it is now one of the most exquisite gardens in Paris, and a representation of the district. Visitors can enter through the grand wrought iron gates decorated with gold. Exploring the park, one can find many delightful surprises: a plethora of statues, a Renaissance archway that was once part of the former Paris City Hall, magnificent trees, a wide variety of birds, and a large pond. Parc Monceau is surrounded by luxurious buildings and lavish mansions, including the Musée Cernuschi (Museum of Asian Arts). It is a tranquil and pleasant park that is visited by both Parisians and tourists. The park also has playgrounds for children.

Printed in Great Britain
by Amazon

25369474R00050